Chocolate Sauce is a boutique publishing company for children. Our company philosophy promotes the importance of looking within to find fulfillment and meaning in one's life.

Enriching children both big and small, Chocolate Sauce books are designed to nourish the soul, brighten the spirit, awaken the mind and warm the heart.

Our exclusive author's boutique is a melting pot of creative, like-minded individuals awakened to the wonders of life and intent on doing some global good.

At Chocolate Sauce we believe in the importance of having fun!

The Now I Know collection helps kids young and old solve real life issues in today's complicated world by bringing the wisdom of ancient teaching into a fun and contemporary format.

We hope you enjoy this book!

Sincerely,
Chocolate Sauce

For more information, please visit:
www.chocolatesaucebooks.com

Enriching children both big and small

ISBN 978-0-9740268-8-6

NOW I KNOW...

That it's better to keep quiet about the good things I do.

by Sally Devorsine

For my two daughters,
Anwen and Sujata.
May they become true heroines.

THE DALAI LAMA

ENDORSEMENT

Geshe Langri Thangpa (1054 —1123 CE) was a Buddhist master famous in Tibet for his 'Eight Verses of Mind Training'. He originally wrote them down for his own personal use, but they have later become an invaluable guide for many other practitioners down the centuries. The proof of their worth is that these practical instructions on how to make oneself and others happy in everyday situations are just as relevant today, for both adults and children, as they were nearly 1,000 years ago. This I can say from my own experience, for I myself was introduced to them when I was a young boy and I have recited them every day since then. When I meet with difficult circumstances, I reflect on their meaning and I find it helpful.

Sally Devorsine teaches English in Bhutan to the young reincarnation of a lama who was one of my own esteemed teachers, Dilgo Khyentse Rinpoche. She was inspired by the verses of Langri Thangpa to create these colourful storybooks, initially to entertain her young student. Later, she realised that they might provide a way to introduce some of the longstanding values that we Tibetans hold dear to children elsewhere in the world today.

If we are to ensure a peaceful future for our world, I believe that it is important that we foster positive values like compassion, kindness and love in our children's minds from an early age. Certainly books like these can help us do that. Each of these stories shows the young reader a different way to secure happiness, whether it is by recognising anger when it arises, being aware of how our every action has an effect on others, or looking beyond our first impressions of people we meet.

I congratulate Sally Devorsine on her efforts and hope that these charming books have the edifying result she intended. I am sure they will delight readers young and old.

: used to think
: was a hero.

. even modelled
yself on Robin
ood.

. was ruthless
championing
ne rights of
ne poor, the sick
nd the lonely.
n fact, I used
) seek them out,
ctively searching
r good deeds to do...

But it was my little sister who was the true heroine...

I just didn't know it at the time.

was too busy wanting
veryone to like me...

was too busy doing things
ke cycling my friend Timmo
o hospital, after a bee stung him
n the eye.

Oh my goodness Charlie! Thank you, my dear. So sweet of you!
or taking lots of sweaters to the lady next door who was always shivering in her garden chair...

The nest must be around here somewhere...
There was the time
nursed a baby bird
days, who had fallen
a tree.
friends
so impressed!

And the time I gave three young kids from my sister's class some secret exam techniques because they were falling so far behind in their studies.
Charlie's so cool...

nd when Class B got upset because they wanted a rabbit ke Class C instead of a guinea pig, I exchanged them. mazingly, Class C didn't even em to notice!
Thank you so much, Charlie! You're the best!

And when Esme was lat
for her piano lesso
I borrowed Ryder
go-kart and we drov
as quick as lightnin
through the farmer
fields to ge
there on tim

It was really muddy!

HERO
I started to like the shine
in people's eyes when they
spoke to me, with awe....
They even made me a t-shirt
with "Hero" in big letters
on the front.
I wore it with pride.
I must admi
the whole thir
was kind of addicti
and I loved it.
I started to show off ar
take risks, I started to ta
too much and bra
I tried harder and hard
to be the good gu

When Megan's brother was sick,
I remember finding lots of toys outside a
shop on the high street and taking
them to him in hospital.
They really cheered him up.

It wa
almost a
if I wa
untouchabl
invincibl
beyon
judgement..

or was I

ne time, I
ent hours
the youth
lub, making
rocket for
eo's baby brother
ho needed some distraction
om his chickenpox...
t took an awful
t of glue,
aint, string and
ape and it was
uite a mess.
WAS going
tidy up,
t I left in
rush...
d when I came back at the end of the day,
the room was spotless.
glue
Who did that

Another time, I took Mo for a walk by the river because she was feeling glum. But as soon as we arrived, she remembered she was supposed to pick up her baby sister from nursery.
Oh gosh, you've been so kind Charlie! But I really should get back now...
We ran there as fast as we could, but found out her sister was already at home!

: started to wonder...
ho had tidied up the youth club?
ho had picked Mo's sister up from nursery?

: found myself
niling shyly at
veryone I met,
hinking maybe
hey're
he one'.

: stopped
earing my
ero shirt.

:t seemed a bit
oo tight.

tchy.

Meanwhile, I noticed my little sister was becoming more and more busy, I hardly saw her...
And when I did see her, she seemed so tired.
Her eyes were blank and void whenever we looked at each other over breakfast.
She was spaced out.

Slowly I began to put two and two together and I devised a plan to test my theory. I took some gnomes from Mr. Engels front garden so Tom could draw them for his homework project.

When he was finished, we put them on the patio and went into the kitchen for a drink. Then I peeped from behind the door.

Sure enough tiptoeing onto the patio came my little sister.

She grabbed the gnome and sprinted back to Mr Engels garden with them.

She placed them neatly all in a row, exactly as I'd found them.

So, I questioned her.
Why?
Just because...
Because what?
Erm...
Because what?
Because I see you making everyone happy, and it's great!
oh, Thanks!
But I also see all the work you leave behind...
The work?
I can show you if you like...?

I had to run around for hour
trying to find out whose bike it was tha
you'd borrowed to take Timmo to hospita
so I could replace it before it was missed.

You just left it there at the hospital, in the car park

And you're lucky you didn't see the upset on Mom and Dad's faces when they discovered all their best sweaters had disappeared!
told them
was me
nd I did a
hole week
chores
round the
ouse to say
rry.

And you thought the ba
bird had just flown awa
but actually I re-united hi
with his poor squawkin
mother (who was
distraught
after searchin
for her f
day

nd I don't think you really thought about all the
nildren who'd studied so hard for their exams,
nose marks became lower because you helped
nree lazy ones to cheat?

owned up to that too, took the blame and made sure they
t the marks they deserved...but spent a whole week in detention)

Then there was another week's detention for pleading guilty to swapping the rabbit and the guinea pig!

(The children from class
had cried uncontrollabl
all day long when the
found their belove
rabbit was missing.

Not to mention
cleaning up Ryder's
go-kart which
was full of mud
and cow-dung
and grass.
I was starting
to understand...

Did you ever think about the poor boy working in the toy shop who lost a days wages because he was on duty when you took all those toys to cheer up Megan's brother?

(I worked a week in that shop, after school, to make it up to him)

or Leo's younger
ister who was
lso needing
istraction
rom chicken pox?

(I made her a
princess doll)

Suddenly it all made sense.
My sister had seen what I hadn't.
sure that I am the
bla-di-bla who can
I went there and the
me who bla-di-bla
sure that I am
bla-di-bla who
I went there
me who bla-di-
that I
oh no.
Don't worry, it's ok. I was happy to do it all. Really.

bla-bla because I am the only
er that I of course bla-bla
I bla-di-bla and of course
Hm-hmmmm...
HERO
I'm cringing now
to think how I
used to come home
every day
bragging about
all the good deeds
I'd done...

And my sister
never said a word.

Instead, the whole
time she'd been
secretly picking
up all the pieces
from the mess
I'd left behind.

I think, somewhere along the way, I had lost track of what "Hero" really means

A hero should be someone who can see the bigger picture, the consequences of every action, how one thing affects another...

Someone who can then tie up all those loose ends, alone, with no complaints and no hope of recognition.

My sister is the real heroine

I offered her m t-shirt, but she just laughed out loud!!

So, I threw it in the bin

I still try my bes to help other but I'd like to thin I know mor about how it shoul be done no

A little bit extra at the end...

1. What does the word "Hero" mean to you?
2. Do you have any heroes or heroines? Why do you admire them?
3. Have you ever tried to help someone and it went all wrong?
4. Make a chart with four columns. The left hand column is titled "Charlie's good action", then "The consequence", then "Hazel's fix-it solution", then "A better original plan".
5. Think of five good actions you could perform over the next week. Try to consider them from every angle to make sure no side-effects will occur. Then plan to do everything in secret. Make a report as you go along.
6. Charlie liked to help others because he saw how it made others look up to him and like him. Why do you think Hazel liked to help others?
7. Who do you think got a deeper, longer lasting sense of satisfaction from helping? Is there a line in the book which tells you this?

In short, may I, directly and indirectly
offer happiness and peace to all
my mothers.
All their harm and suffering
may I secretly take upon myself.

Langri Thangpa (1054–1123)

With thanks to Khyentse Yangsi Rinpoche for the handwritten verses.

This book is one of a series of eight books
from the "Now I Know..." series.

Each book is based upon one of the eight verses of mind training
written by the 11th century Tibetan Buddhist master, Langri Thangpa.

Each verse, written in the back of the book, offers a different method
for finding happiness, both for ourselves and for others too.

Now I Know...That I wouldn't be who I think I am, without other people.

Now I Know...That I'm not, actually, Mr. Wonderful.

Now I Know...That it's better to face my monsters.

Now I Know...That we all have a jewel inside us somewhere.

Now I Know...That I should pop my balloon before it gets too big.

Now I Know...That silly hopes and fears will just make wrinkles on my face.

Now I Know...That it's better to keep quiet about the good things I do.

Now I Know...That I just have to keep my eye on the ball.

Sally Devorsine left her English roots behind many years ago... She now lives high up in the mystical eastern Kingdom of Bhutan. Nestled in the foothills of the Himalayan mountains, Sally has spent the last ten years teaching young Bhutanese, Tibetan and Nepalese monks the ways of the western world (including all the subjects you love to hate!).

With this 8 book collection, Sally seeks to bring some of the thin, crisp air of Bhutan to your boggle-fogged modern mind and give it a brisk spring clean through with stories inspired by some of the amazing pieces of wisdom she has heard along the way.

In this book, Charlie learns that to truly be a Hero, we have to let go of WANTING to be a Hero!

Sally (Sky Laughter) is an author in the Chocolate Sauce book boutique.

Now I Know Collection
Retro Cool Wisdom 4 Kids.

Made in the USA
Las Vegas, NV
30 November 2024

12911998R00026